IF YOU WERE A...

Veterinarian

IF YOU WERE A...
Veterinarian

Virginia Schomp

BENCHMARK BOOKS

MARSHALL CAVENDISH
NEW YORK

Hungry raccoons, friendly chimps, nervous farm horses, curious iguanas—all kinds of animals need the veterinarian's care.

If you were a veterinarian, some of your best friends would walk on four legs. In a busy week, you might shake paws with a hundred kittens and pups.

Imagine giving a shot to a hissing snake. Or asking a gorilla with a toothache to "open wide." Would you like to feed a bottle to a baby raccoon? Could you wrap a bandage around a two-thousand-pound bull?

Each day would bring surprises from patients of all shapes and sizes if you were a veterinarian.

Vets enjoy working with animals and teaching people how to take good care of them.

This doctor's waiting room is always filled with noisy "babies." Most of the babies have furry ears and tails. That's because the doctor is a veterinarian. Veterinarians take care of the health of animals the way your own doctor takes care of people.

In cities and large towns, vets mainly care for small animals. Most of their patients are dogs and cats. Peek in the veterinarian's office and you also might see a pet guinea pig, rabbit, hamster, bird, turtle, or snake.

Not all pets are cute and cuddly!

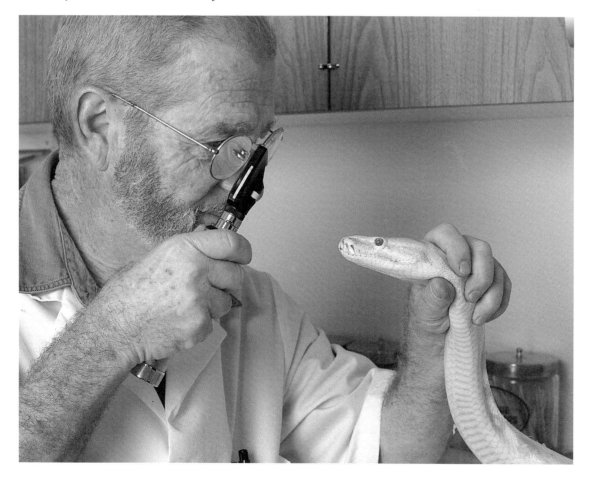

Checkups will help keep these kittens in "purrfect" health.

The veterinarian's most important job is helping healthy animals *stay* healthy. If you were a veterinarian, you might have fun examining these small kittens. Their wet noses quiver as you check their eyes and ears and listen to their heartbeat and breathing. You weigh each wriggly pet and take its temperature. Now you know these new patients are off to a healthy start.

At each doctor's visit, animals are weighed to see how fast they grow.

Next up, a cat whose teeth need cleaning. Animal doctors are animal dentists, too.

Some pets are here for their yearly checkups. For others, it's time for vaccinations (vak-suh-NAY-shuns). The animals don't always like these shots, but the medicine will keep them from getting some serious diseases.

Just like people, animals can get cavities if their teeth aren't kept clean.

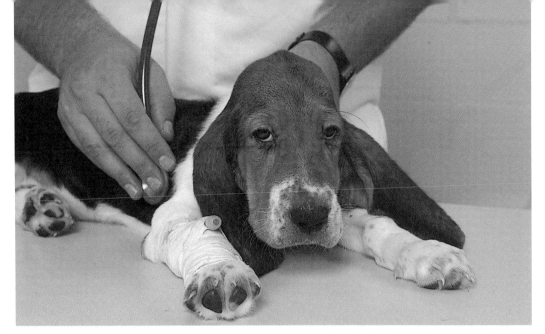

When a pup loses its pep, a stethoscope helps the vet find out what's wrong.

Shots can't stop all diseases. And a sick animal can't say where it hurts. That's why a good veterinarian is also a good detective.

The doctor-detective's weapons are medical instruments. With a stethoscope, the vet can listen for problems in the heart and lungs. A thermometer tells the patient's temperature. A microscope spies out tiny germs.

The veterinarian pieces together all the clues. The mystery is solved! The vet knows why the animal is sick and how to make it better.

Even a cat can have a CAT scan, a test that lets the vet see inside its body.

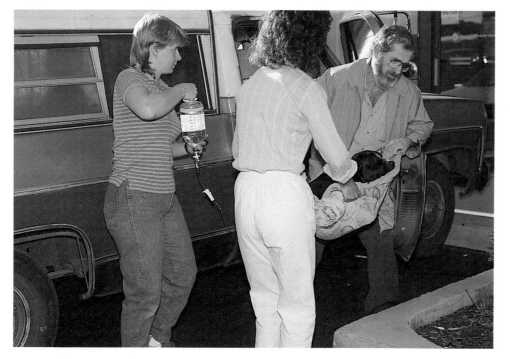

An injured dog is rushed to the animal hospital.

Emergency! A dog has been hit by a car. An X-ray machine takes a picture of the inside of its leg. The picture shows a broken bone. The vet will have to operate.

Cutting open the leg, the doctor screws a metal pin inside the bone. The pin holds the broken pieces together. A cast wrapped around the leg will keep it straight while the bone heals.

The operation takes two hours, but the patient doesn't mind. Thanks to a drug called an anesthetic (an-us-THET-ik), the dog sleeps through the whole thing.

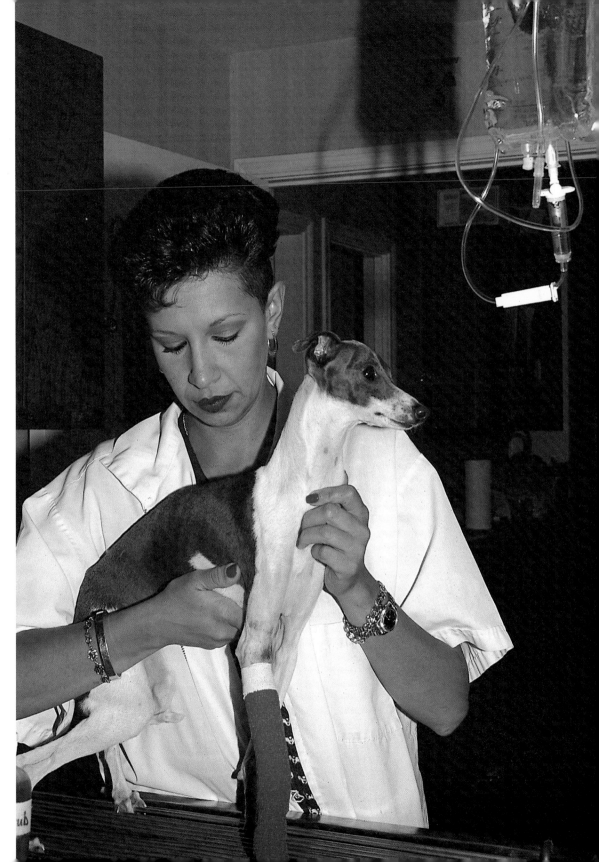

In a few weeks, this pup's broken leg will be as good as new.

The vet's firm, gentle hands calm a nervous colt.

Picture a herd of cows stomping around a waiting room. If you were a country veterinarian, you might want to visit some of your patients at home.

Most country vets spend part of each workday at their office, treating pets. The rest of the time, they drive to stables and farms. Their office travels with them. Some vets pack their cars or trucks with a thousand pounds of supplies. It takes lots of tools and medicines to be a good doctor to hundreds of cows, horses, pigs, sheep, and goats.

This farmyard goat gets regular checkups, just like a city cat or dog.

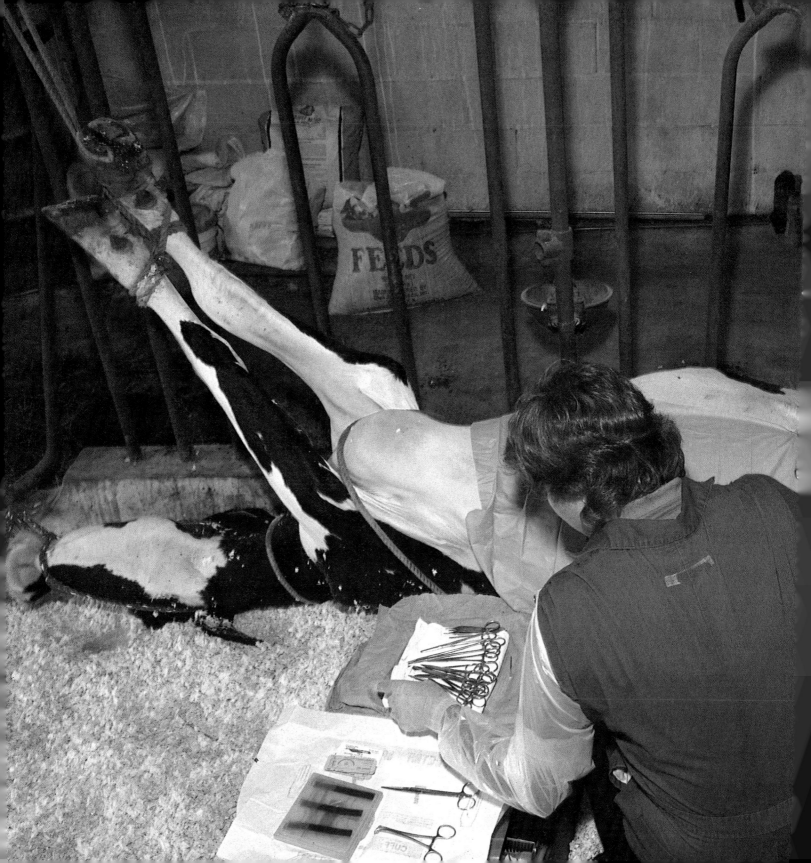

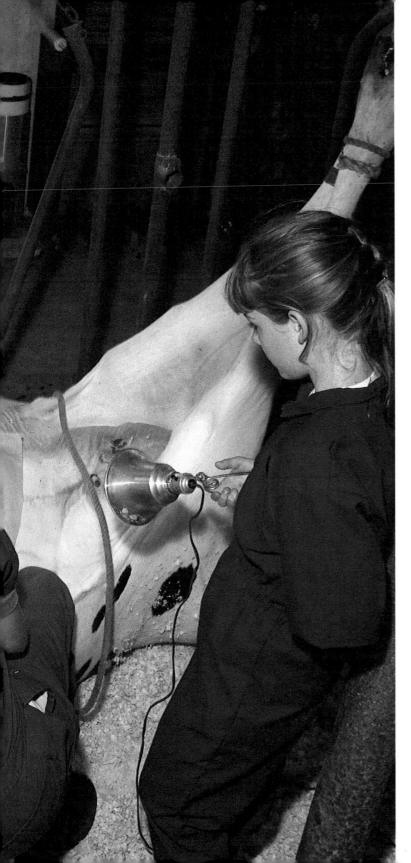

Baby goats must have their horns trimmed. Horses need their teeth filed. Cows can get sore feet standing in muddy pastures. If you were a country vet, you would know the special needs of each farm animal.

The phone rings before sunrise. During the morning's milking, a farmer has found a sick cow. You hop from bed and hurry to handle the emergency. In a chilly barn, you operate and save the animal's life.

With her daughter's help, a vet performs an emergency operation on a milk cow.

Strong arms help a calf come into the world.

The next emergency call may mean a new mother needs help. Most animals give birth easily, on their own. But sometimes the vet must help pull the baby out of its mother's body.

Animal mothers know just how to take care of their newborns. Again, the doctor lends a hand. Vaccinations protect barnyard babies from disease, and vitamins help make them strong.

In less than an hour, the newborn is ready to take its first steps.

Wild animal babies sometimes need a doctor's help, too. A wildlife veterinarian may raise an orphaned animal until it is old enough to live on its own. How would you like being a substitute mom or dad to a baby raccoon or opossum?

A few milk drops make a meal for a tiny opossum.

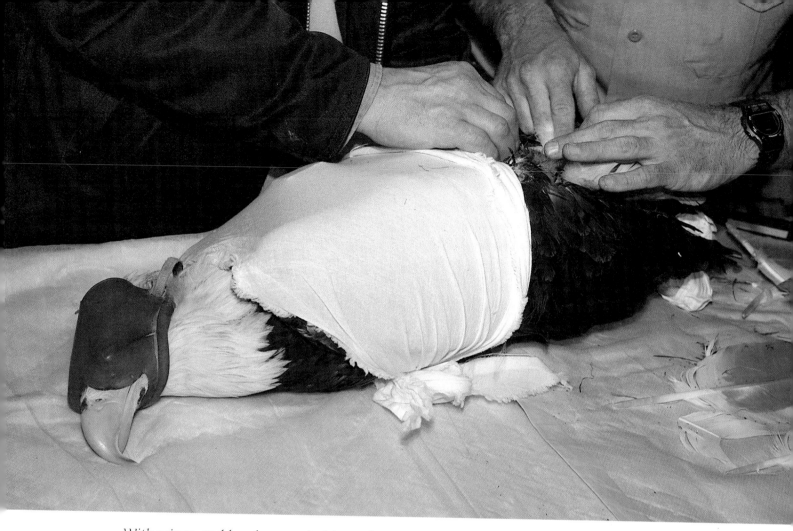

With wings and head covered, this eagle can't hurt itself or its doctors.

Maybe you'd rather spend your days with bald eagles and polar bears. Some wildlife vets camp out in mountains, forests, and snowy fields to study how wild creatures live. What these vets learn helps us to protect wild animals and their natural homes.

Wild animal parks copy the natural homes of *really* wild animals—lions, tigers, elephants, and other visitors from faraway lands. It's not easy caring for thousands of different kinds of animals. Vets at wild animal parks and zoos must be clever, gentle . . . and careful.

Clever thinking can trick a fussy animal into taking its medicine. Gentle hands help the vet examine the fragile legs of a baby deer or giraffe. And wouldn't *you* be careful if you had to give a gorilla a checkup or pull sore teeth from a lion's mouth?

Special drugs keep an African lion sound asleep in the operating room.

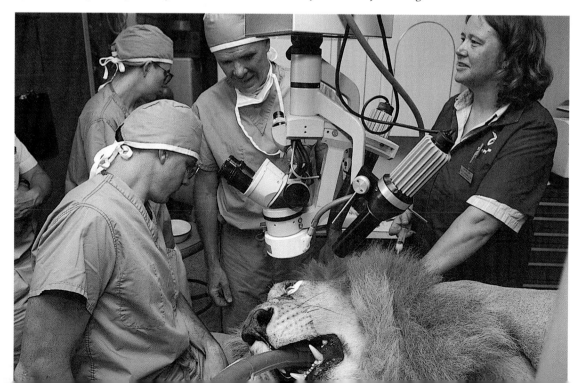

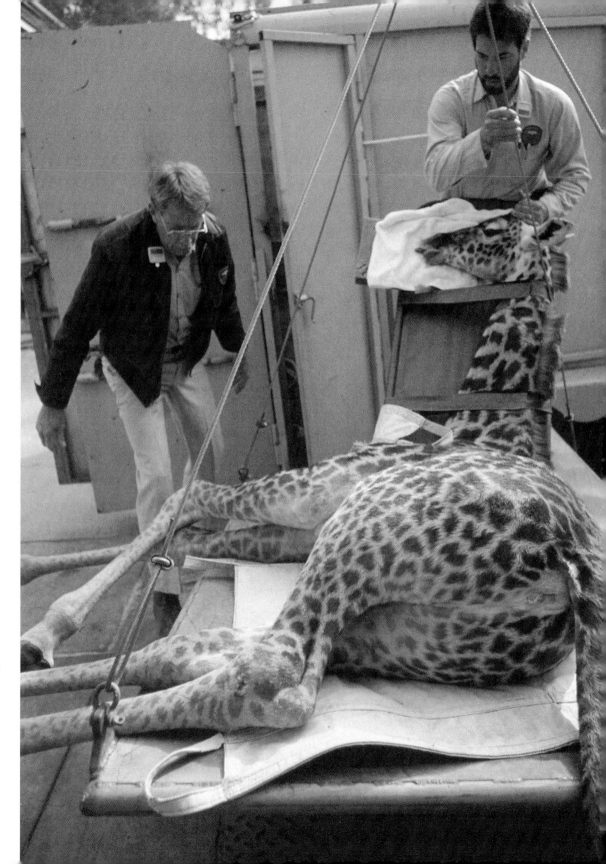

To move a baby giraffe with a sore leg, zoo doctors need an extra-long stretcher.

To become veterinarians, students must learn all about animal medicine.

How do veterinarians learn to care for lions and giraffes, cows and horses, dogs and cats? They go to veterinary school after college. There they study the way animals' bodies work. They learn about different diseases and how to treat them.

Do you get good grades in school? Do you love animals? Would you work hard to learn how to heal them and keep them well? If you answered yes to all these questions, you could be a veterinarian!

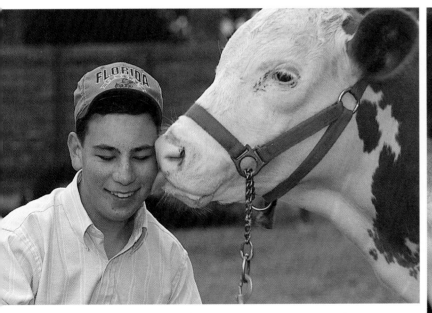

Most of all, future vets must love animals.

VETERINARIANS IN TIME

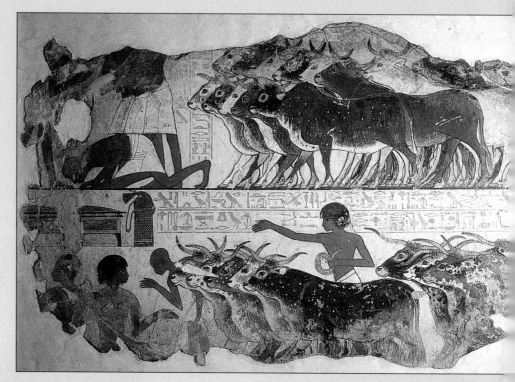

Animals have always been important to people—even 3,400 years ago, when this painting was made on the wall of a tomb in Egypt.

Doctors have studied veterinary medicine for thousands of years. This painting comes from a book on animal care published around 1400.

A veterinarian in the late 1800s treats a lady's pet dog in his shop.

French scientist Louis Pasteur, who lived from 1822 to 1895, developed vaccines to prevent animals from spreading dangerous diseases.

In the 1900s, an animal ambulance brought free doctor's care to pets in poor parts of London, England.

A VETERINARIAN'S CLOTHING AND INSTRUMENTS

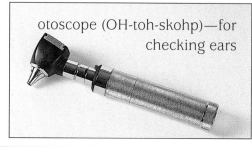
otoscope (OH-toh-skohp)—for checking ears

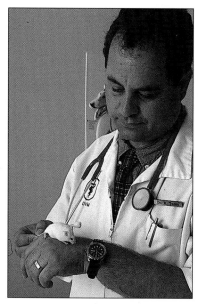
A lab coat keeps the vet's clothes clean in the office.

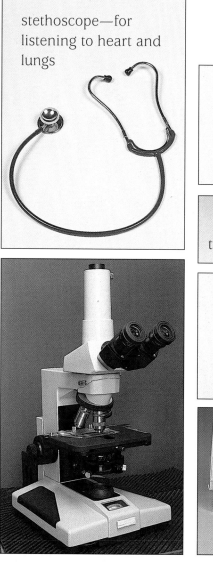
stethoscope—for listening to heart and lungs

scalpel—knife used in operations
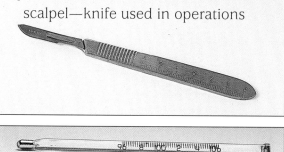

thermometer—for taking temperatures

ophthalmoscope (ahf-THAL-muh-skohp)—for checking eyes

microscope—for looking at tiny things

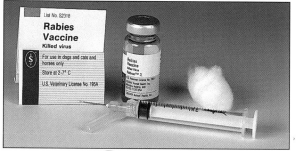
vaccine—for preventing disease; syringe (suh-RINJ)—for giving shots

Overalls and boots protect clothes in messy barns and pastures.

WORDS TO KNOW

anesthetic (an-us-THET-ik)   A drug given during an operation so the patient will not feel pain.

microscope   An instrument that makes tiny things, such as germs or parts of the blood, look larger.

stethoscope   An instrument used by doctors for listening to sounds inside the body.

vaccination (vak-suh-NAY-shun)   Giving a shot of a medicine called a vaccine (vak-SEEN) to keep an animal or person from getting a disease.

X-ray machine   A machine that takes pictures of the inside of the body.

Benchmark Books
Marshall Cavendish Corporation
99 White Plains Road
Tarrytown, New York 10591
Copyright © 1998 by Marshall Cavendish Corporation

Library of Congress Cataloging-in-Publication Data
Schomp, Virginia, date   If you were a veterinarian / Virginia Schomp.
p.   cm. — index.
Summary: Describes the work of veterinarians, who deal with many kinds of animals.
ISBN 0-7614-0613-1
1. Veterinarians—Juvenile literature. 2. Veterinary medicine—Vocational guidance—Juvenile literature.
[1. Veterinarians. 2. Occupations.] I. Title.
SF756.S36   1998   636.089'06952—dc21   96-44277   CIP   AC

Photo research by Debbie Needleman

Front cover: *Norvia Behling*

The photographs in this book are used by permission and through the courtesy of: *The Image Bank*: G.K. & Vikki Hart, 1; HMS Images, 31. *Norvia Behling*: 2, 4 (top left), 5, 6, 7, 8, 9, 10-11, 13, 16, 22, 27 (left), 30 (top left, top center, top right, second from top right, second from bottom right, bottom right). *Zoological Society of San Diego*: Ron Gordon Garrison, 4 (top right), 25. *Photo Researchers/The National Audubon Society Collection*: David Frazier, 4 (bottom). *The Picture Cube*: Eric Millette, 12. *Animals Animals*: Norvia Behling, 14. *Steve Bentsen*: 15. *Catherine McDermott*: 17, 30 (bottom left). *Henry Horenstein*: 18-19, 20, 21. *Peter Arnold, Inc.*: John Cancalosi, 23; Matt Meadows, 26; Leonard Lessin, 30 (bottom center). *Phoenix Zoo*: Dick George, 24. *Mark Needleman*: 27 (right). *British Museum, London/Werner Forman Archive/Art Resource, NY*: 28 (top). *The Pierpont Morgan Library, "Livre de chasse," detail, M.1044, F.31V/Art Resource, NY*: 28 (bottom). *National Library of Medicine*: Mark Marten, 29 (left). *Mary Evans Picture Library*: 29 (top and bottom). *Tufts University, School of Veterinary Medicine*: 30 (center right).

Printed in the United States of America
1   3   5   7   8   6   4   2

INDEX